$8 1195

THIS HOUR *of the* TIDE

SALMON PUBLISHING LIMITED

receives financial assistance from the

Arts Council/An Chomhairle Ealaíon.

•

CATHERINE PHIL MacCARTHY

THIS HOUR *of the* TIDE

SALMON  POETRY

First published in 1994 by
Salmon Publishing Ltd,
A division of Poolbeg Enterprises Ltd,
Baldoyle Industrial Estate,
Baldoyle, Dublin 13, Ireland.

© Catherine Phil MacCarthy, 1994

The moral right of the author has been asserted.

A catalogue record for this book is available from the British Library.

ISBN 1 897648 19 7

All rights reserved. No part of this publication may be reproduced or transmitted in any form by any means, electronic or mechanical, including photography, recording, or any information storage or retrieval system, without permission in writing from the publisher. The book is sold subject to the condition that it shall not, by way of trade or otherwise, be lent, resold or otherwise circulated without the publisher's prior consent in any form of binding or cover other than that in which it is published and without a similar condition, including this condition being imposed on the subsequent purchaser.

Front Cover Painting 'Treasure I' by Mary Rose Binchy
Back Cover Photograph by Ann Egan
Cover design by Poolbeg Group Services Ltd
Set by Poolbeg Group Services Ltd in Palatino
Printed by The Guernsey Press Ltd,
Vale, Guernsey, Channel Islands

for my mother and to the memory of my father,

and for Justin

Acknowledgement is due to the editors of the
following publications in which some of these poems
have appeared:

*Poetry Ireland Review; Krino; The Salmon; Stet;
The Irish Times; The Irish Review; The Connaught Tribune;
Fortnight; A Sense of Place; The Farming Independent;
Irish Studies Review; Orbis; Field; The Sunday Tribune;
The Seneca Review.*

Catherine Phil MacCarthy's poems have also appeared in
the anthologies *Women's Work* and *Six for Gold*
and have been broadcast on RTE Radio 1,
The Arts Programme and *Sunday Miscellany*.

Contents

III

I

Barley Sugar

My mother washed the eggs with bread soda,
strained milk through a flour bag
into a scalded can,
sent us wrapped in coats and scarves
vying for who would venture first
elbow deep in meadow grass
out across the hayfield
over the wall at Hannon's
to skirt past the collie,
shiver as a door unlocked.

Still in a dressing-gown
she would turn to take
fresh eggs and milk
slowly to a new fridge,
ask us to stand in
out of the rain,
pin her hair back,
then lead us to a darkened
bedroom and we would follow
in a pool of wonder
to peep at twin baby daughters,
ask again to see her galoshes,
ease three rings
down her long slender fingers,
before chasing up to the wall
clutching barley sugar
as the dog barked,
our coats caught in briars.

And I would trail
behind my sister,
forgetting all about our hurry,
crouch down to pick
cowslips in the damp,
reaching for white stems
to lift tiny ragdoll shapes,
vaguely pluck a flower
suck the stamen for honey,
and find myself lost in the meadow
with nobody left to follow,
straggle home late for breakfast,
pinafore laced wet
to greet my father
outside our back door
with eggs in his upturned hat.

Killing the Bird

One refused to die.
Her long white neck
wrung from his knee
where he sat
in the middle of the yard,
a snowstorm of feather and down,

trying to hold
yellow claws to his lap,
her throat drawn with the other hand
so tight, blood dripped
bright red, human
from her beak.

I looked on
disowning his nerve,
thinking, not for all the gold on earth
could I, as the strain
distorting his mouth
showed me

the struggle was personal
to the final twitch
of snowy breast plumage
when her neck
tumbled from his knee
like mink.

The Rose

I remember a hot tear-washed face,
spring cabbage leaves
cut from young heads

simmering on the stove,
how the raw light
exposed her broken veins

and gathering up scraps
in bare hands
how afraid we were of slugs

and how we laughed;
when I looked to offer a hand
the hush of a big shower

darkened the house.
Alone I traced raindrops
down a window pane,

crushed petals in my palm,
water from a rose I picked
streaming in my hand.

The Thrush's Nest

He aimed at my lap.

Plums landed in my dress,
ready to wash
at a rainwater tank.

Our steps matched to the spout.
Rushing water held our hands,
then I said

I'll show you the bird's nest.
We raced to the bank.
Our fingers touched twigs, moss, feather.

Three speckled blue eggs
slid from his palm
into a pocket.

Apart we ran to the garden gate.

Leavening

From a worn silvery tin
I peel dough
to rub between my palms
into rats tails or worms,

while you knead and turn
on a base smooth as a rink
what sleeps between your fingers
pliant as a child's limbs.

You sprinkle an oven plate,
dip the knife in water,
then slice across twice.
Dough sags in lifting hands,

the oven door closes.
I learnt to tell time
by that baking swell of heat,
forgotten at the last minute

we rush for a cloth
and whose fault if it's burnt
as you rap the crust?
In a waking city,

a child at my breast,
I look at the face of a clock
for soda bread wrapped in a linen cloth,
and the window fogged up.

Making Hay

I stole glimpses of
his adam's apple, bare
collar bone, a forest of wiry curls,
held at the margins of a world
by winks and acrid jokes.

He drops on one knee
to secure a stack.
Creosote fumes from twine
in his hands nicked
with a penknife or snapped

at a sole of a leather boot.
I enter his world with a look.
Beneath my palm your chest is
fur, then silk
stops at the fragrance

of hay, fresh cut,
falling evenly from
the blade behind the horse,
ripe seeds not yet
surrendered to the earth.

The Black Field

One day in summer
father was called from the meadow
and that night your sister
covered the dressing-table mirror
in fear of what she might see.

Three of you slept together
trying to forget the red
emulsion on his jacket sleeve
when he walked into the yard white
and you couldn't read

in his face what he'd seen.
Three of them, big men,
filled the kitchen,
a bottle of whiskey between them
and your mother made tea

talking about how
she was odd in her ways
and hadn't been to Mass for years
though a lift passed her gate every week.
The children played

pretending not to hear
how she went that morning
to count the cattle,
never came home for dinner,
and what was she thinking

when she took off her boots
and left her nylons draped over,
a woman of her age
finding the grass wet beneath her feet?
The rushes and even the bog iris

must have held her,
for it was how they came across
an apron swollen on the water
after calling and calling her name
in every corner of the fields.

Stone Circle

The first bra pinched her ribs.
Away from the house
down the worn cow-paths,

she pulled a stalk of
flowering ragwort in her hands
and smelt hot earth.

Opened glass buttons of a blouse
let broiderie anglaise
fall to the grass,

lifted a slip over her head,
unfastening a bra
with one hand.

Afraid to be seen by a man
she offered young breasts
to the sun.

She found a place to lie
in a hollow of the mound,
for company,

buttercups,
a solitary oak,
an abandoned ring of stones.

The Laundress

She's ready to go in
but needs to catch her breath.
One or two things remain
to be draped across the line.
It leaves you time
to chase white butterflies

fretting over sweetpea
your mother coaxed
on the chicken wire
you bend towards
closing palms
on pollen-dusted wings

you want to show her,
slowly opening hands,
but she's already gone
past the silver trails
on the leaves of cabbages,
the gate keening on its hinges,

nowhere to be found
in the front yard
where ribs of a washboard
drip stars on the lintel.
Inside and out, the house
is empty, awhile ago

noisy with linen
dropped on the stairs,
hands flushing bloodstains
in salt and rainwater,
suds from the tub
streaming over the kitchen.

Next thing you know,
late afternoon she sits down
to rest and you are the child
asleep on her lap.
Or she drowses and you
count freckles on her breast,

instead of sheep
running from her path
in the early morning
when she comes to help
your mother with washing.
Or you are the woman

giving yourself
to the heat
of another's kitchen,
meeting the nut brown
of her eyes when
she places a cup in your hand,

before making a way home
past the hazel in the horse's field
to bathe small children
by the stove, holding them
in the same bare light
you left them in.

Earth Bound

On a clear evening
a child down the fields
imagined waves
lifting on the horizon
in rifts and billows of cloud.

Perched on a stone wall
she tucked a smocked dress
tight between her knees,
holding her breath
for the ocean to sweep over her head,

with no notion of years passing,
returning home
a woman longing
to press her ear to the shell
of a whitewashed wall.

Magnetic Field

At the bottom of the bog,
I lost my bearings:
Everything I had to go on

for a map, the shimmer
of poplar and birch
against the evening sun,

our small stream,
gorse shrubbing the bank,
disappeared with a squelch of my rubber boot.

I was knee deep
in a seepage of mud and peat,
among rushes and yellow flags.

No one to be seen for miles,
except horses in the next field
grazing under pines,

tales of a man
swallowed whole and never seen again
fresh in my ears.

Everything that was
air and sky in me
sucked in mud at my heels

and everything in me
that loves the bog
praying for rock.

Going to Knock

Long before he took me
all the way on the train
with Paddy Clohessy talking
about the county team,
calf prices that spring,
cows giving the best milk
(we knew them all my name),
their conversation mellow

as an old whiskey,
I used to take down
the tiny glass basilica
from the white mantelpiece
in my parents' bedroom
and shake the water inside
to watch snow fall
in a blizzard over shoulders

of men and women
on a pilgrimage for sins,
and stand still in the room
when the electric light
blinked and dimmed –
the moment of apparition –
hearing an ocean sway
in the branches of a pine,

knowing it's dark
by starlings rummaging
in eaves of the barn
and the tick of a yard-light
is my mother going out
to close the hens,
asleep on one leg,
on the rungs of a shed.

Rag Doll

Straw-haired. Patchworked. I am
the rag doll you threaten to lose.
Each time, you push me

into the dark under the bed
to see if I'll be lost
when you turn blindly groping

cobwebs. Sometimes you slap me
on the face and warn
that I have to be good. Once,

you even tried to strangle me,
the vice grip of your small fingers
on my throat so fierce, tears

dripped from your eyes. At night
I sleep next to you on the pillow.
Your eyelashes brush my cheek.

Soon I'll be gone forever.
Neither of us will know
exactly how it happened.

Hunger

His outstretched hand grasps
thin air above the wall
to stop falling
and the yard comes up
to meet his whole body
hungering for oblivion.

Out cold for the last time
in the haggard
after digging
a few stalks of potatoes,
the burning pain
will take him
to the roots of an apple tree
where swallows
on a wire before dark
steady their ruffled feathers
against winter.

He holds on
to the sheets in bed
drunk on the wet-mulch scent
of a young woman who isn't there

light amethyst in the window
of a room darkening
round his head.

Sweet Afton

Burnt incense at my throat,
the flicker of a brightening candle,

I watched the priest
raise a scrupulous hand,

to swing the silver thurible.
A row of heads bowed.

And going home in the car
my father dipped headlights

and slowed to enter our gate
past a black Morris Minor

backed to the grassy river –
Reilly's hand ventured under tweed

all the way up nylon stockings,
coming to grips with

the fluid insides of thighs,
her head thrown back,

she inhaled a Sweet Afton –
unaware of a passing car,

the wide eyes of a girl
in darkness closing a gate

held by the red light
of a cigarette.

Knock Fierna

His quietness was all of
sixteen, New Year's Eve.
Tense shoulders
held me on the way home.

Kilmeedy, Ballingarry, Croom,
Knock Fierna behind us
in darkness,
we snailed along icy roads.

Tail lights up ahead
loomed close.
Like a runaway horse
the old green Volks

swerved in and out of fog,
taking both sides of the road,
and I was awake and yawning
on the first hour

of nineteen sixty-eight,
after my first dance,
watching the moon rise
over Ballycahane bog

and the crazy driver in front
slumped over the door,
any minute about to
capsize in the ditch.

Burning Bushes

October I see you
heaping bushes in a sheltered spot,
sleeves rolled up,

shirt open at the neck,
coat slung on a pitch fork.
Frost pierces the earth.

Slowly you strike a match,
dip light in three places,
your hand on my shoulder

draws me back from the sparks.
We watch it catch,
small twigs snap first,

seeping woodsmoke,
then a whoosh and bushes burst into flames.
I place my hand in yours

knowing we'll stay,
drink hot tea as the sap weeps
while flames turn blue

and night falls
on our land of milk and honey,
and the only light left

when the first stars rise
is light from the fire
burning away the years.

Lady Chatterley

We curled on the stairs
outside 'Sacred Heart',
talking after lights out –

Lawrence, Mansfield,
Virginia Woolf,
our first love.

That world would startle
with nuns on the prowl
or the shock of our voices

become one
like a sudden bright moon
flooding the stairway;

six floors down,
a grandfather clock
in the convent hall

ringing each small hour.
Sleepless bones creak
getting up to leave,

night-gowns we shrug close,
your hair falls blonde on my skin
with the whitest touch

placed in my hand,
and beautiful you are gone
leaving me

wordless
on a precipice,
hugging the forbidden book.

The Bull Calf

I slipped from the bed,
gathered up my clothes,

went barefoot downstairs,
to dress by the stove.

In the yard my father
was hitching the trailer.

I sipped tea unable to
swallow buttered toast,

went out to load calves
in the dark, found myself

putting together stars
the shape of teddy bears,

an up-turned saucepan
strewn over the horizon,

the Plough, the Milky Way,
a cluttered nursery,

and bringing me to sanity,
the little bull

with white markings
making an escape beside me.

At the market,
dealers swarmed creels,

cupped the lit ends
of cigarettes to their palms,

felt the rumps of calves,
asked how much,

walked away
with a shower of insults.

Bloody free country,
we called to their backs.

Here, a man said, finally,
spitting on his hand,

'Will you shake?'
I rubbed my calf,

curled in hay,
my fingers frozen to the nails,

seeing him in a strange field
at evening,

refusing to
drink from the trough,

the mother at home
lowing for days.

II

The Island of Adventure

The underground passage
became so black
we could hardly see.
I gripped your hand,
led us on, excited at

feeling my way in the dark,
George and Julian
on the trail of a mystery
inching blind to where
the walls were almost visible,

the rock hewn above our heads
seeped. Our feet
came to a halt
where the floor disappeared
a couple of hundred feet deep

like the well at home
we lay on our bellies
to peep in.
Light at the bottom was
no sky with our heads in it

and no headlong pebbles
hit water
wrinkling the mirror.
The white explosion of
the sea in a tunnel,

timed like dynamite
to go off at intervals,
daubed the quiet
and dizzied our senses.
Beyond the drop,

a passageway tempted us,
heartbeats louder
than our breathing,
the whole cliff around us
absorbing the shock.

Ballycotton Bay

We never crossed the stepping-stones
to the island at low tide
to watch red boats
out coasting for sharks.

Instead we turned from the sea
and strolled back-roads in the heat
to Shanagarry.

We never saw the ocean run with blood,
the man lean out, cast
his spear through water.

Coming home along the coast
to sleep in a single bed,

we found the tide in,
and the strait between island and shore
a rush of treacherous water

and in the middle of the bay
the chug, chug of a boat
with a halo of gulls

black cargo in tow,
torn flesh blanched in salt water.

The Opal

The jeweller in New Hampshire
turned opals on his palm,
focused a telescopic light
strapped to his forehead
on milk-white, blue-green, crimson,

like a miner at a seam
exploring a vein
along its length with fingertips
or working deep in the hill
to touch cracks in ironstone.

One he called fire
showed a hair-split
invisible when turned in the light
as the ocean bedrock at the Flaggy Shore
impinged with sunset

where we sat against the wall
kissing in the warm dark.
The air was silent assent.
A chain slid on my neck
and you retrieved the clasp.

I looked down
knowing a day might come
when I would turn
to see half the opal gone
or the entire stone.

The Gift

Lily of the Valley
shoots arrived in clumped
earth on my doorstep
that November,
a walled garden
in a cardboard box.

I went looking for
leaf-mould, mist, heat,
out the back with no hope
in an overgrowth
of brambles, nettles,
broken terra-cotta pots.

Under a boundary wall
an overhang of vine
they found a home
inside a rotting log
bleary-eyed with mushrooms
and vanished.

Winter left only
ribbed grass
where I came across them
in late May, scented pearls,
closed to everything
but rain.

The Omen

Under the bridge
at Lansdowne the cormorant
sank her blueberry snake's head
in rainy waters of the canal,
coming up further down
an eel in her mouth,
thick rubber
curling at both ends
she dips and slaps
in the air
chewing its spine
to a string –
she gorges
the middle first
moving down river
to rest in the shallows,
her neck the sleek
bulge of a serpent
high above plane leaves
devouring tail feathers.

Sanctuary

Last thing at night
we go down a stone path
in the cool of a cliff

to cross a lip of sand
that hardly ever catches the sun,
entered as it is and stretched

by the barnacled tide.
Our low voices start
high above our heads

the muffled shrieks
of a colony of kittiwakes –
children dancing on spring beds –

quiet when we pass
the blinding globe of light
where the pier begins

and our way is lit
over frayed cable
soaking a puddle of oil.

Rows of clinkered boats
rock softly side by side,
and halfway down

a creel of fish stinks
beside stacked lobster pots
rigging the pitch horizon

which in a few hours will be
dawn beyond the lighthouse,
its extravagant flare

now wheeling once, twice,
and then the black
stillness of stars.

Those bright seconds tell us
like lost sailors
where we are,

and when the moon comes
from behind that cloud,
you show me the swell

driving towards land,
between the third
and fourth hour of the tide

always hardest to navigate,
and the salt spray on my lips
a farewell to

the sanctuary of cliffs
where high up the very rock
heaves with birds' nests.

New Hampshire Lightning

Drops spatter my hand
as I lean on the rail of the porch
looking across at the barn.

Low clouds above the wood
sieve down and you are calling me
to come in

when thunder shells the roof.
A deer wanders below the tree line,
sniffing rain from the apple bough

before turning to look
rooting me to the spot.
Later when lightning electrifies the pines

our table goes black,
I search the dark for your eyes
and find the forelegs of a deer in flight.

Artichokes

From early summer
their sage heads
intricate as a mosaic,
swelled to
infant cabbages
like three we picked

when you came,
flirting and peeling
ivory leaves
to dip in melted butter
and tease shy flesh
between our teeth.

The rest got spiked
purple hair
the week you left,
tips festering
to a pincushion
blue and remorsefully

hanging their necks.
By November our world
was shrunk
to a brown withered husk,
hearts turning to
skeins in my hands.

Ballinamona Park

i – The Lake

We walked the rim
in search of the swan.
Sometimes our path ran out

or straight into water,
left us scrambling over roots
of wild rhododendron.

What I envisage now is
not that wetland you brought me to,
darkened with floating leaves,

calyces of lilies
and the orange heel of the swan
paddling brackish water

but the lover who rose
years and years before
and flew into a live cable,

her luxurious whiteness
crashing through air
feathers awry,

and you and me falling
deeply in love
with disaster.

ii – Wheat Field

As if you were a Fitzgibbon
taking me over the home place.
Silk waist-coat
made you a gentleman
pointing out the lodge,
the loyal gardener

and round the back
one summer evening
we stood in an empty stable
looking past cultivated fields
for horses grazing
in pairs and threes.

Underfoot the gravelled yard
carried us all the way
to the roadgate
through sea-green fields of wheat
deep enough to ripen,
green enough to make love in.

Birth Mother

That Christmas she asked for photographs.
Without parents.

I checked the last roll
of film developed,
feeling her eyes

smart along a sleeve
all the way to a tiny fist.
That first glimpse

she risked over hot whiskey
in the quiet of a bar at closing-time,
silken brown hair slipping over

an inextricable love
the wide river of her breath

sparkling with red leaves,
intertwined limbs,

her heart breaking all over again
in the white turmoil
of rapids.

Mimosa

Lemon flowers
lift out of mist
for the first time
since I put it in –

a fern-like slip,
sensitive to minute
changes in temperature –
half to see it

weather the worst frost
and half to mask
the concrete igloo
in a neighbour's garden.

Once a smoking house,
fed by an underground channel
or a furnace for baking
unleavened bread

in the Middle East
eased out of fire-ovens
on a flat shovel.
Mrs Kempster said one day,

"Look, the old bomb shelter.
Built all across the city
to escape Hitler."
Now, this flourishing tree

exposed to the sky
hiding people
running from the house
when the bombs are falling?

The Lost Tribe

That week-end we turned a corner
bereft of tribal shelter

walked a medieval street hand in hand
to lean on a bridge of the Corrib,
our faces exposed to east wind.

White rapids surged through the city
towards the open sea
where a bitter sky turned blue,

and the red boat of my childhood

lowered one summer to a stream
danced from my hand to float away,
slowly taking water

was the listing hull at Anach Cuain
full of children's screams.

Hurricane Winds

A parents' row
bitter in the small hours,
but by morning the sky clear,
going its own way in little gusts,
a hush in the kitchen
after breakfast
when he passes her chair,
laying his great hands
wordless on her shoulders
and she letting them
rest there a moment,
gets up to clear the table.

A day or so after
I found the wall down
beneath the russian vine,
and just stood
watching the breeze
haul a veil of leaves
between me and a neighbour's garden,
slow to see the loss:
a summer of ox-eye daisies,
rings of cyclamen buds,
lily of the valley.

Anaconda

Together we look at
Kahlo's self-portrait,
the long neck adorned by a grass snake,

her head wound with plaits
on a background of leaves,
on her shoulder, a black monkey.

You point at the picture
and say, Mama.
Her eyes dare me to see.

On a pedestal
a huge serpent
coils flank upon flank.

My fingers trace
live curves,
wary of its power,

the way my mother at
an Easter procession,
paused before the crucifix

to press her hand to
the feet of Christ.
I half expected to feel

more than bruised metal
gliding from my hand
the killing heat of the tropics.

Buddleia

It broke my heart.
Pushing clusters of
blue flowers
in our faces at the gate.
We could hardly breathe.
Time and again I cut back
the strongest shoots
with sécateurs.

You hated it,
made several attempts
to dig out the root.
When I got home one day
you were sawing it like a tree.
So many butterflies.
Rusty blossoms
trailed the grass.

We hacked at the stump,
gave up. I saw you
rig the car-jack in place,
then wind it up.
Our child came running in,
called me to see:
earth all over the place.
Your boot resting on the spade.

A black tangled mass.
Unearthed. Like a heart.
I thought of
photographing it,
turned it over and over
like an old tooth:
To hide in a safe place
keep bad spirits away.

Nativity

We kiss and when you
leave for work
I notice the figures

you made of modelling clay
red, green, blue, yellow
all over our house.

The night before
you lovingly moulded shapes
to stave off grief

hands worrying flesh,
all the care you took
taunting me with loss.

The Wooded River

Hand in hand we wandered
past the drowned forest,
mudflats scattered with herds,
shallows and deep channels.

You followed me on a dirt track
through groves of oak, ash, hazel,
a sweet herbal cool,
wild mint, honeysuckle.

You came to me in a field of tall grasses
rippling in the wind like barley,
white butterflies fretting
over the reds of poppies.

Birth of Aphrodite

I carried you to the tideline
holding you over the water
to dip small pink feet in a breaking wave.

Our toes eddied with roselight.
A grey haired couple found themselves
paddling side by side.

The sun burned red below slate ridges
and time settled into colour.
Refractions of a sapphire ocean,

mother of pearl insides of
a scallop shell safe in my pocket
and nothing in the world to reveal

heartbreak in the purple confines of
the Dublin mountains
and your weight in my arms.

Vendetta

A granite valley,
the son called
to uphold family honour,

sounded the criss-cross
rhythms of
an edging stone

for the mantra
of a savage killing,
the night he went out

to hunt down
his father's assassin,
in the heat

of that moment
knowing his life
had one meaning.

New Moon

Your eyes,
violet pools
at the kitchen table,

a mountain spring to
swim nude in
breathless with

the shock of
cold water
gripping my skin,

spilling down
sandstone rocks
in the heat

under pines,
you take me
into the night

a new moon,
Jupiter
at her side.

The Last Night in France

We stayed up late.
Shutters closed.
Dark wood of a country table
between us. Your daughter

asleep upstairs. You rolled
cigarettes. Each one lit off the last
sent our conversation
adrift in every corner of the room.

Even from here I know
that garden smelt of lilac and rain.
We quenched the lamp
and climbed the stairs

with no fears in a strange house
but I was all night caged
in the air of a child's room,
before the lightning.

Quicksilver

When the frayed silk
of our silence breaks,
talk is a thread

where all the pearls
have spilt in tiny pools
like mercury I once chased

across the floor
to catch fluid grains
vanishing in a dusty crevice.

Springtime in Clare

When arctic winds
lacerate the Burren,
old hill keeps her head down
cradling Alpine blue
gentian budding in her veins.

Exorcism

Nothing prepared me for
the change in your voice.
The story of how

you buried her little girl,
surrendering to the grave
in the small coffin

your own birthless years.
April swept rain from the headland
and ditches inclined

whitethorn buds
and not a soul knew
your dreams were

chrysanths scattered
from your hands
on the raised earth.

Mamo

from *Bailegangaire*

Hair spread on the pillows,
talking to yourself,
as if words are
ways of settling debts

and the spinster daughter
waiting, tense, for
the pound of the stick
on the floor upstairs,

is the child you hit
on the head with a curse.
She stamps out her cigarette
when the time comes

urges you to the story's end
with the sure hands
of a midwife
delivering a birth.

The Wound

I brought you my hand
severed at the wrist
but for skin:

Aphrodite fled from the wars
after bidding to
rescue her son,

stands before
the woman dressing that wound
silenced by

her judiciousness,
no longer feeling hurt,
only numb again,

straining to
break into words
re-member what happened.

Looking for Pearls

Just when I'd walked town
looking for a string of pearls

in the mirrored corners
of antique jewellers

a woman unlocked a glass case
handed me the only one

for you, a coiled glow
that slinked across my fingers.

She showed me how
to tense knobbed silk

and grit the beads along my teeth
telling everything

of mollusc and stone
on the Great Bight.

I made up my mind
left the shop

a chill of live oysters
on my tongue

just when I'd found
what I wanted to give,

but you'd already
moved on.

Japonica

I almost told him why,
a lighted alcove,
a table underneath a stairs,
in someone else's house,
the japonica spray,
I was unable to tear myself away.

I almost told him why
I went out to take cuttings,
knelt by a wall
in April rain,
flowering shoots
in my gathered skirt,

a memory of hurt fingers:
Wet kindling
taken home to dry
seeped by a fire,
fragrant where it
caught light and spread.

I almost told him
why I braided my hair.
Petals fallen
round a tracery of branches
lay untouched
in a circle of flame.

Magic Circle

You gave me a book
in the sitting-room
with light pouring in
and mountains
I've seen in all weathers,

leafless winter,
the fire banked with red coals,
air so chill our breath is
smoke, and over-night
snow patching grey slopes.

Time came full circle
that afternoon in summer,
when the tortoise raced the hare
and the crab moved sideways
across an ocean floor,

the children went out,
left us to the quiet of a house,
the sun still high
and no sign of
day drawing to a close.

Touching Down

When your flight touched down
did I ever tell you
I was coming out of Bartletts
antique shop at Ringsend Bridge
that Christmas after buying
five black and white
china kittens for my niece?

The street trembled with
jet noise. A seagull lost
altitude and buffeted,
went into a perfect glide.
Clouds over the city
turned to brine.
A juggernaut roared by

reminding me of Tenth Avenue
and Eighteenth, a flat
on the corner, shaking
to the foundations
into the night.
I tossed and turned unused to
intense heat and noise.

I leaned over the waters
at Ringsend and closed my eyes
to imagine you standing there
and my feet moving against
the earth's pull.
For a whole minute I held you
in my arms, hold you still.

The Crossing:

i – Metamorphosis

For weeks afterwards you heard
seagulls and the farewell hoot
of a ship downriver. The day
you stood on the bridge watching
a liner turn from the quay,
you were writing a story. Words
always caught at the same point:

A small tug reins the hull
in a wide arc across
the full width of the river.
The baulked motion of the keel in water.

ii – The Blackbird

For three days I heard the wing-beat of
a blackbird trapped
in the chimney breast,

that flutter of feather against brick
a wild attempt to rise.
I slept and woke, the scrape

so thin and haunting in the end,
that it was me, crying,
please let me out.

Raise me from this blackness
to the light. Let me fly
straight up through the chimney-well

to rove again the skies of London.
Green squares. Magnolia
open in white flames.

And I will show you a place
where the hawk hangs
glorious

and when we hear rapt stillness
we'll know
the blackbird is dead.

iii – Wilderness

I never go back
not even in sleep
to that place you called ours,
edge of the wilderness,

where two cedars touch the sky
and high at the brow
a glider soars
then drops over plains.

I never go back
where the sun lures the breeze,
and we sprawl all afternoon
talking wild dreams,

not even in sleep
when your lips brush my hair
and your voice
is a whisper of lions,

to this place you called ours
with fire in the air,
where surf licks
the whitest beach.

iv – The Crossing

You took the glasses from the shelf
poured us each two thimblefuls

and moved your easy chair to mine.
Our knees were almost touching.

Your eyes held mine
steadfast over the roll and pitch

of conversation and once again
a ferry rolled beyond

harbour waters into the first deep
troughs on the open sea.

v – Playing with Fire

All summer I worked at night
alone in a white room,

the throb of rafters cooling
and over the wild garden
behind our house

noise of a truck
pulling up in the creamery
and milk stacked to
the rhythm of a man singing.

His voice teased
the dewy rhododendron
woke the birds,
brought me to light with a flow of words.

I went downstairs
to open the door
and stand in fresh air
looking down-river at a mist
curled on tidal water

that later lifted in haze
enveloping trees
where children played with matches,

hours after I undressed
to settle in your embrace
your hand cupping my breast.

vi – Voodoo

That Sunday I took a train to Rye
and tried to escape the sun,
lying alone in the damp
shade of a breakwater,
a row of sleepers
half-eaten by salt-water

on a verge of marram,
reading my book,
the same sentence
over and over a riddle,
eventually shaking my head
to dislodge you
from my ears like water.

The wood was bleached,
and cool to touch
as the air of apple orchards,
one midnight we drove there
and walked cobbled streets,
you showing me

the dark cross-beams of Tudor houses.
I lay back,
the sleeper, a totem
against a lava blue sky,
bringing us to the wild
shores of my own country –

a spray of red roses on the seat
as you drove away in the car –
and thought of you,
nothing but you,
the whole day.

vii – Dreamtime

All winter he was
inside me
in the blood-orange room,

damask curtains
that let in
the baby blues and pinks of

West London sunsets
and when I woke
dazzled by ice and snow

I picked my way to the tube
past stalls laden with
melon, yam, kumquat.

viii – Camille

She went to him late that evening
the day of Victor Hugo's funeral.
He held her gloved palms
the veiled fever of her smile

sent the model home
closed the studio door.
Wordless she turned
to take off her clothes,

entered
the circle of his eyes
neck inclined
to the tremor of his lips.

He kissed the white
between shoulder blades,
his tongue to the small
curves of her back,

both of them lost,
clay in their hands
at the sudden
beat of the angelus.

ix   Attic Room

Down the line dark is falling.
I walk to the end of the platform.

Iron tracks gleam after rain.
Late clover on the bank.

A bird sings. Orange streetlights
coming on will soon burn

that blue to indigo,
but not before a star's light

in the tunnel glows
and separates into headlights

of a fast underground train
taking me to a June afternoon,

when I sit with eyes closed
speeding to the moment

I mount the stairs to an attic room
and find you,

shirt unbuttoned at an open window,
watering geraniums.